Weather

Thunderstorms

by Brienna Rossiter

FOCUS READERS

SCOUT

www.focusreaders.com

Focus Readers is distributed by North Star Editions:
sales@northstareditions.com | 888-417-0195

Produced for Focus Readers by Red Line Editorial.

Photographs ©: Sasa Prudkov/Shutterstock Images, cover, 1; jctabb/Shutterstock Images, 4, 16 (top left), 16 (bottom right); Anna Om/Shutterstock Images, 7; Minerva Studio/Shutterstock Images, 9; Jeff Gammons StormVisuals/Shutterstock Images, 11; Grisha Bruev/Shutterstock Images, 13 (top); Suzanne Tucker/Shutterstock Images, 13 (bottom); Alexey Stiop/Shutterstock Images, 15; Dan Tautan/Shutterstock Images, 16 (bottom left); Mara008/Shutterstock Images, 16 (top right)

Library of Congress Cataloging-in-Publication Data
Names: Rossiter, Brienna, author.
Title: Thunderstorms / by Brienna Rossiter.
Description: Lake Elmo, MN : Focus Readers, [2020] | Series: Weather | Audience: K to grade 3. | Includes index.
Identifiers: LCCN 2018060798 (print) | LCCN 2019002430 (ebook) | ISBN 9781644930106 (PDF) | ISBN 9781641859318 (ebook) | ISBN 9781641857932 (hardcover) | ISBN 9781641858625 (pbk.)
Subjects: LCSH: Thunderstorms--Juvenile literature. | Severe storms--Juvenile literature.
Classification: LCC QC968.2 (ebook) | LCC QC968.2 .R67 2020 (print) | DDC 551.55/4--dc23
LC record available at https://lccn.loc.gov/2018060798

Printed in the United States of America
Mankato, MN
May, 2019

About the Author

Brienna Rossiter is a writer and editor who lives in Minnesota. She loves learning random facts by reading books, going to museums, and traveling to new places.

Table of Contents

clouds
lightning

What Are Thunderstorms?

Thunderstorms bring rain.

They have dark **clouds**.

They have **lightning**.

Lightning flashes.

We hear a sound.

The sound is thunder.

How They Form

Air rises.

The air cools.

It forms a tall cloud.

Rain falls.

The cloud is cold.

Ice forms inside.

Bits of ice float.

Some bits crash.

The crashes

cause lightning.

Kinds of Thunderstorms

Storms have strong wind.
Small storms bend plants.
Big storms break trees.

plants

tree

Storms bring rain.

Some rain freezes as it falls.

It forms **hail**.

hail

Glossary

clouds

ice

hail

lightning

Index